A note to parents, grandparents, teachers, and others:

Discover Devils Tower National Monument is written for elementary school children. Educational information, ideas, and participatory activities are presented in a fun, light-hearted manner to engage and encourage creativity and learning.

Devils Tower National Monument covers an area of 1,347 acres near the center of Crook County in northeastern Wyoming. *Discover Devils Tower National Monument* explores the natural and human history of Devils Tower National Monument. Adventures and historical events are covered, as well as the natural wonders that abound. Young children can learn to appreciate our precious natural resources and help to preserve them for future generations.

Written by Bobbi Fischer

Illustrated by Steve Parker

Produced by American Educational Press
a division of Phoenix Publishing Group
4113 N. Longview
Phoenix, Arizona 85014
www.phoenixpublishinggroup.com

ISBN 1-881667-00-6
Printed in the United States of America
Copyright ©1992 by Devils Tower Natural History Association
All rights reserved, including the right of reproduction in whole or in part in any form.
Second printing

TABLE OF CONTENTS

Discover Devils Tower National Monument

Geology of Devils Tower National Monument 4-5
American Indians 6-7
Indian Legends 8-9
History of the Name 10
Early Explorers and Homesteaders 11
The First National Monument 12
Historical First Climb 13
Technical Rock Climbers Today 14
Famous Parachutist 15
What Is It Like on Top? 16-17
Prairie Dog Town 18-19
Belle Fourche River 20
Hiking Trails and Safety Tips 21
Pine Forest and Life Zones 22
Wildflowers 23
Birds of Devils Tower 24-25
Wildlife Mammals 26-27
Snakes of Devils Tower 28
Poison Ivy and Safety Tips 29
Recycling 30
New Words 31
Answer Page 32

GEOLOGY

A long time ago northwestern Wyoming looked very different. The climate was warm and wet, much like the tropics today. Shallow seas covered much of the land. Mud and sand built up on the bottom of the seas. As time passed, the water drained away. The mud and sand were cemented together forming **sedimentary** rocks.

Great pressures deep within the earth caused **faults** (cracks). This pressure pushed the rocks up. They formed the Rocky Mountains and Black Hills. High temperatures melted rocks deep in the earth. Some of the melted rock (**magma**) forced its way up creating volcanoes. Some of the magma cooled and hardened underground forming **igneous rock**.

The igneous rock that makes Devils Tower is called **phonolite porphyry**. The word "phonolite" is like "phonograph" (record player). The rock got this name because it makes a ringing sound when hit with a hammer. Five small buttes are located about three miles northeast of Devils Tower. These are called the Missouri Buttes. They are also made of phonolite. These buttes may be connected underground with Devils Tower

Devils Tower is unique and mysterious. It has four, five, six, and seven sided columns. These columns formed as the magma cooled underground and hardened. As it cooled, the magma shrank in size and cracked. Because it didn't cool too fast or too slow, these cracks met to form columns.

Devils Tower was buried for millions of years. During that time, the weather and Belle Fourche River wore down the sedimentary rock. The softer sedimentary rocks were carried away, leaving the harder igneous rock. Slowly, Devils Tower began to show. The tower stood taller and taller as more rock was washed away.

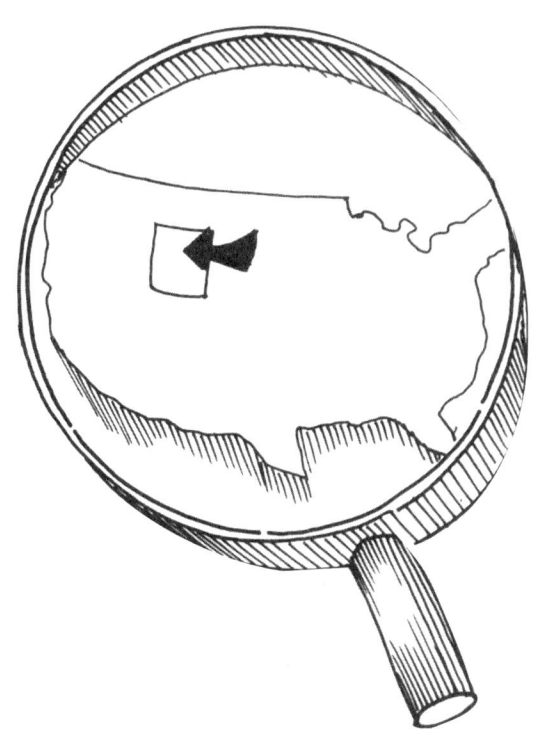

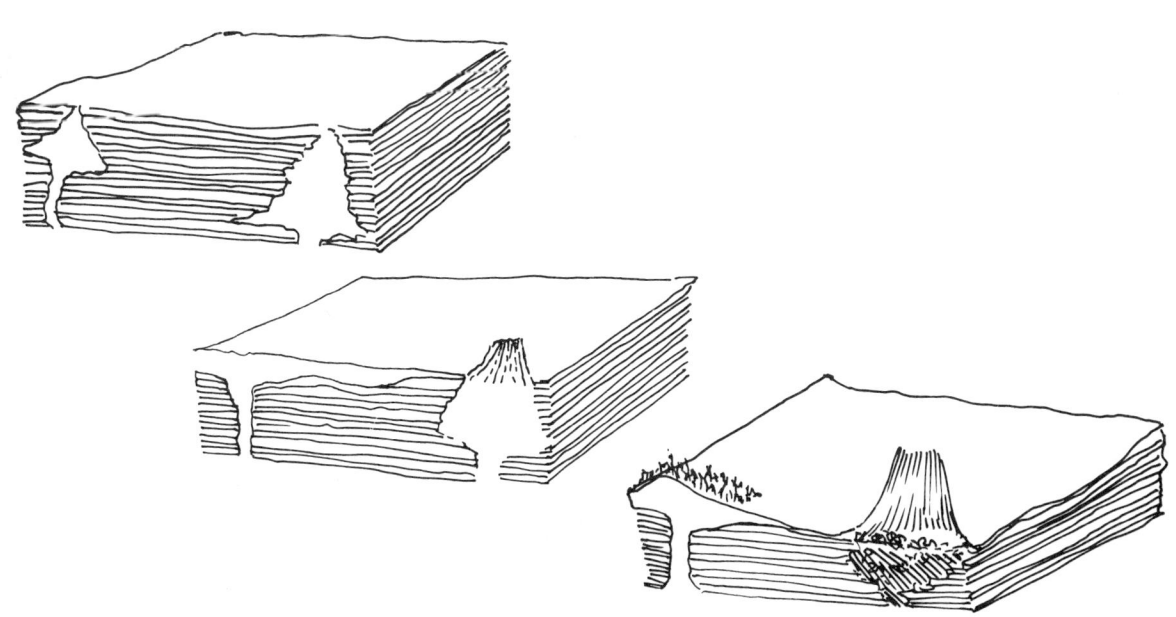

American Indians

American Indians were the first to experience the awesome power of Devils Tower. The Lakota Sioux of the Plains referred to Devils Tower as Mateo Tepee, which means "Bear Lodge."

The tower is sacred to the Indians of the area. Tribes, such as the Shoshone, Kiowa, Crow, Arapaho, Cheyenne, and Lakota Sioux came to fish or hunt buffalo, deer, and other game. They camped in the valley along the Belle Fourche River, but few chose to live there.

The tower is considered a holy place, a place for ceremonies. This respect may be compared to the way some people feel about the Vatican in Rome or the Holy Lands in the Middle East.

Today, Devils Tower National Monument continues to be a place for traditional activities. Personal and group ritual activities include prayer offerings, prayer bundles, sweatlodge rites, and the Sun Dance. Most of these activities appear to be related to the Lakota Sioux tribe.

A prayer bundle is a small article wrapped in cloth and placed in trees or on rocks within the Monument. If you happen to see these bundles, you should not disturb them.

Symbols were used as one form of communication long before our present written language. Pretend there is no written language today. From the symbols provided below, and those that you create, tell a special story just as the American Indians may have done with their symbols.

WRITE A SYMBOL STORY

LIGHTNING	SUN	MOUNTAIN	MOON	BALL	SCHOOL	BOY GIRL
SNAKE	TREE	CAR	FISH	RAIN	HAT	DOG
COMB	BIRD	SHOVEL	APPLE	LAKE	SHIRT	BOOK

INDIAN LEGENDS

Similar accounts of the origin of Devils Tower are shared by many American Indians. Both the Kiowa and the Cheyenne people speak of a giant bear clawing Devils Tower. One version of the Cheyenne legend speaks of seven brothers.

The wife of the oldest brother was carried away by a large bear. The bear took her to his cave. The husband was very sad and would cry to the bear. The youngest brother had great powers and asked his oldest brother to make a bow and four blunt arrows for him. He asked for two red arrows with eagle feathers and two black arrows with buzzard feathers.

All the brothers then went to the bear's cave. At the entrance, the youngest brother told the others to sit and wait for him. He then turned himself into a gopher and entered the bear's den. He found the giant bear lying with his head on the woman's lap. He put the bear to sleep and had the woman crawl through the tunnel to the entrance, after which the hole closed up. The youngest brother turned back into an Indian and they all hurried away. When the bear awoke, he and the other bears, of which he was the leader, followed the Indians.

The Indians arrived at the place where Devils Tower now exists. The youngest brother took the rock that he always carried and asked the six brothers and the woman to close their eyes. He sang a song and the rock grew. He sang four more times and the rock rose to its present height.

The bears arrived and the brothers killed all but the giant bear. The bear leaped at the rock, and each time he clawed at it, he made the grooves we see today. The youngest brother shot three arrows at the bear. The arrows did not harm the giant animal but the last arrow he shot killed the bear. The youngest brother then made noises like a bald eagle and four eagles came to him. The brothers and the woman grabbed the eagles' legs. The eagles carried the Indians from the top of the Tower to the ground.

Kiowa Legend

    The legend of the Kiowa people speaks of seven sisters and one brother. One day they were all playing together when the brother began to change. He grew claws and turned into a giant bear and began to chase the sisters.

    The sisters jumped onto a tree stump. The tree stump rose in the air, far from the reaches of the bear. The bear leaped and leaped at the stump, clawing it with each lunge.

    The sisters were swept up into the heavens and are now the stars of the Big Dipper.

History of the Name

Colonel Richard I. Dodge was in charge of a U.S. Geological Survey party which was formed to explore the Black Hills region. It was Colonel Dodge and his assistant, Henry Newton, who wrote about the uniqueness of the tower.

Colonel Dodge published a book in 1876 entitled *The Black Hills*. He called the peak **Devils Tower**. He explained that the Indians called it "The bad god's tower." Dodge changed that name to Devils Tower. Henry Newton also wrote in his account that the name Mateo Tepee appears on older maps. Newton said the Indians were calling it "the bad god's tower," or in better English, "the devil's tower."

It is believed that the new name of Devils Tower was created after this expedition.

Directions

Complete the crossword puzzle below and on the following page. Choose the correct word from the list on page 11 to complete each puzzle. A letter from each word is given to help you. See answer page.

Early Explorers and Homesteaders

Reports of gold discovery in the Black Hills brought many prospectors to the region of Devils Tower. It did not take long for the gold to dwindle, and homesteaders settled the land.

The Belle Fourche Valley was rich with hilly prairies and spacious grasslands. Settlers from the Midwest took up ranching and farming. A few larger ranches were also found in the vicinity. Cattle flourished, freely roaming on the open range.

Several attempts were made to obtain Devils Tower for private ownership. Fortunately, all were denied, and the Tower remains as a national landmark.

Fill in the puzzle below.

WORD LIST:
Colonel Dodge
Henry Newton
homesteaders
Devils Tower
ownership
prospectors
ranches
expedition
Belle Fourche
Mateo Tepee
Black Hills

The First National Monument

Around the turn of the century, some people were concerned about protecting and preserving areas of beauty and interest. From this conservation movement, the Antiquities Act was passed on June 8, 1906. The Antiquities Act authorized the President to set aside "historical landmarks, historical and prehistorical structures, and other areas of historical and scientific beauty". This created national areas that were to remain unspoiled and protected for future generations to enjoy.

President Theodore Roosevelt proclaimed Devils Tower as the first National Monument on September 24, 1906. Today there are 80 National Monuments.

Solve the secret code below. For example, the letter B is in the \/ and so on. The first letter is done for you.

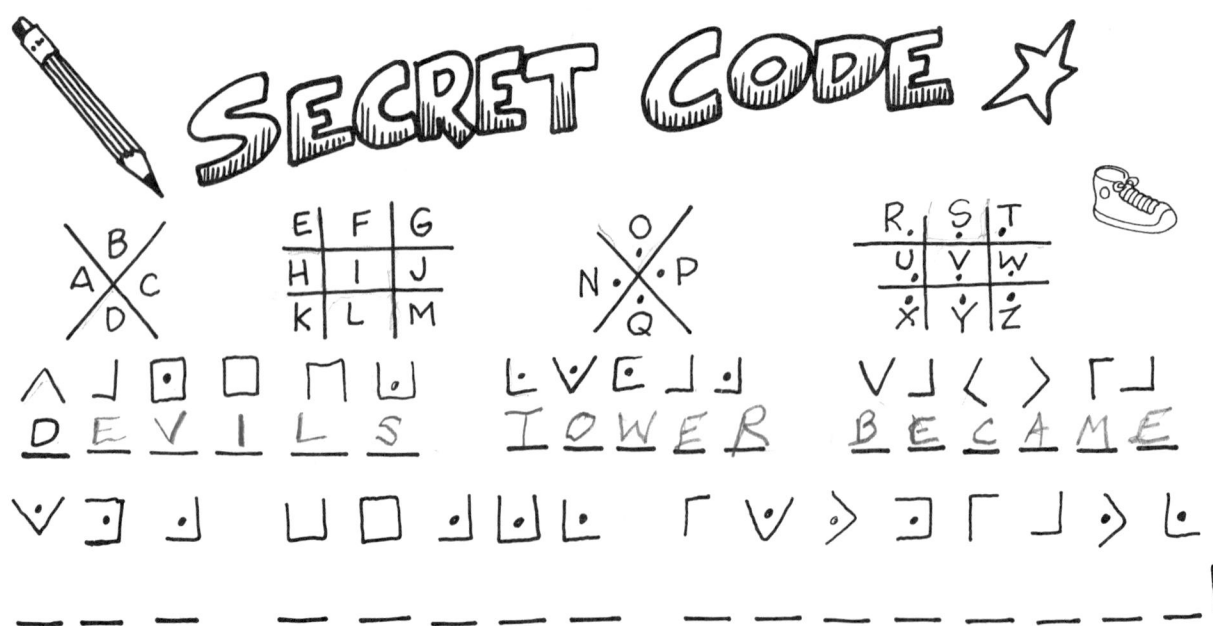

D E V I L S   T O W E R   B E C A M E
T H E   F I R S T   N A T I O N A L
M O N U M E N T !

Historical First Climb

William Rogers and his assistant, Willard Ripley, were local ranchers. They became famous by being the first to climb to the top of Devils Tower. They accomplished this feat by building a 350 foot ladder. First, they drove wooden pegs into a vertical crack on the southeast side of the Tower and then they connected the outer edge of the pegs with a wooden strip. This construction took several months to complete.

The celebrated event, which Rogers and Ripley had promoted and advertised, drew about 1,000 spectators on July 4, 1893. People arrived on horseback or by wagon to watch the famous climb. Many had journeyed several days, covering more than 100 miles, to participate in the celebration.

Rogers reached the top of Devils Tower in about an hour. Before his **descent** (climb down), he staked the American flag, "Old Glory," at the top of the Tower. By afternoon, strong winds blew the flag down. The enterprising stars of the day cut the flag into small pieces and sold them as souvenirs.

Two years later, on July 4, 1895, Mrs. Linnie Rogers, wife of William Rogers, climbed the ladder to become the first woman to **ascend** (climb up) Devils Tower.

You can see portions of the stake ladder today by looking through the pipe tube on the Tower Trail.

Technical Rock Climbers Today

Fritz Wiessner led a party of professional mountain climbers to the top of Devils Tower in 1937. The party completed the **ascent** (climb up) in about five hours. When they reached the top, Wiessner and his party collected samples of rock and vegetation for scientific study.

The next year, Jack Durrance and his party ascended to the summit. Today, the easiest and most popular climb for technical rock climbers at Devils Tower is called the **Durrance Route.**

Most climbing at Devils Tower is **free climbing**. This means that natural holds such as ledges, edges, and cracks are used. The equipment used is a safety system and many items are included for this purpose. Two people are necessary for a climb and this is sometimes referred to as the "buddy system." One partner is the **leader** while the other **belays** (controls the rope by taking in or letting out).

Rappeling is the technique of descending. Climbers "slide" down their ropes which are anchored into the rock. One can slow their descent by "walking" down the rock using a rope through a brake device. Fixed **anchors** (bolts) have been installed in the rock on several rappel routes at the Tower. The climber, therefore, does not have to leave his own gear behind.

Park Rangers share valuable safety precautions and climbing conditions on the Tower with climbers. All climbers need to register with the National Park Service before beginning their climb and they must check in upon their return.

Today, there are more than 225 different routes to explore on Devils Tower. Climbing is safe if care is taken but one must know the techniques of rock climbing and think about safety at all times.

Listed below are several items used by technical rock climbers. Each item is hidden throughout the book. Find each one and write the page number beside the item.

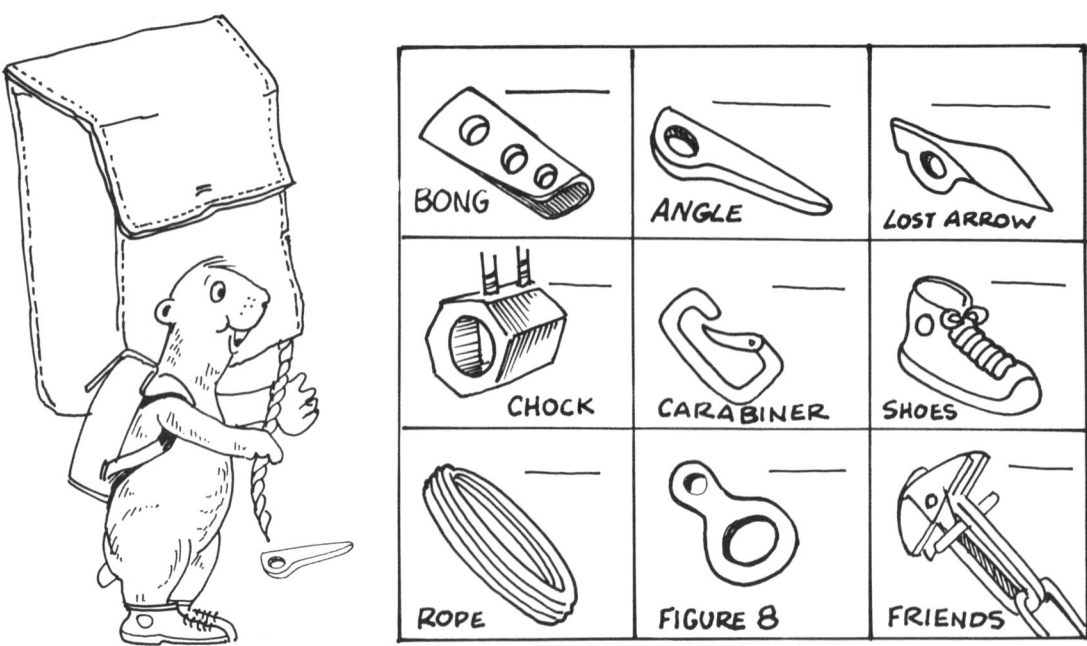

Famous Parachutist

A professional parachutist, George Hopkins, brought media attention to Devils Tower on October 1, 1941. Without the permission of the National Park Service, he jumped from an airplane and landed on the top of Devils Tower. Hopkins planned to climb down using a rope which was dropped from the plane. Unfortunately, the rope landed on the side of the Tower beyond Hopkins' reach. The National Park Service and Hopkins had a problem...how was Hopkins to get down?

Thousands of curious readers learned about Hopkins' predicament through the newspaper. Telegrams and letters of advice on how to rescue Hopkins arrived at Devils Tower. Blankets and food were dropped by plane to the parachutist.

Why didn't they use a helicopter, you wonder? Helicopters were not in common use at that time so another solution was necessary.

After six days, mountain climber Jack Durrance led a rescue mission to the top of Devils Tower. The climbers found George Hopkins in good condition, and they all made it safely to the bottom of Devils Tower. About 7,000 visitors came to watch the famous rescue!

What Is It Like on Top?

What do you think you would find at the top of Devils Tower? Can you imagine finding snakes, packrats, or chipmunks? All of these mammals have been seen at the summit of Devils Tower! This rocky area actually supports many plants and animals that have adapted to its harsh **environment** (surroundings).

How do you think they got there? It is the opinion of some people that predatory birds may have dropped them. Others believe it is more likely they just climbed up the Tower like humans. Many climbers have reported seeing snakes or rodents inching their way up the cracks, too!

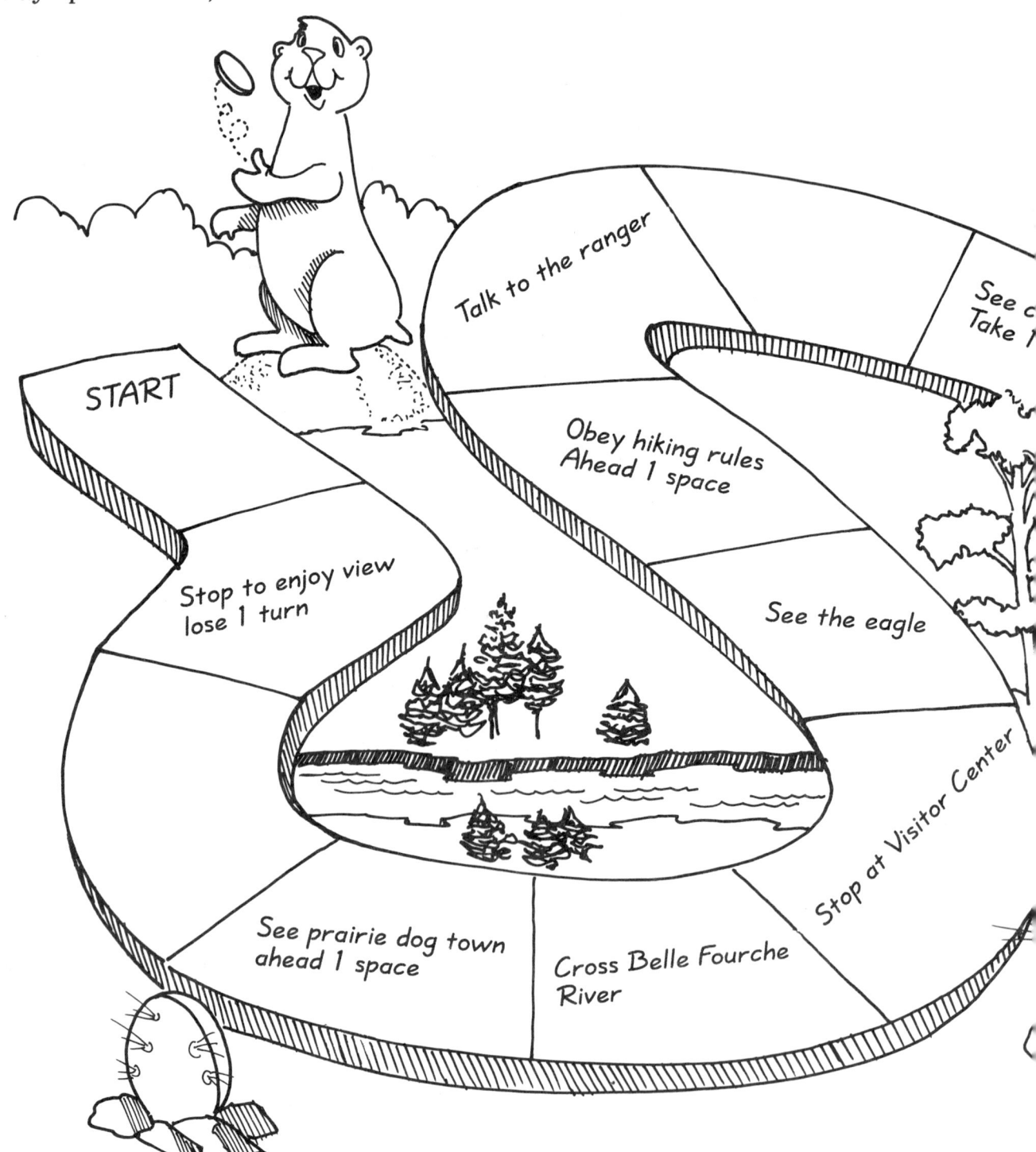

The top of the Tower is not as flat as you might think as you view it from ground level or high up in a plane. The soil is thin, yet several varieties of plants grow there. Many people report it looks much like the surrounding countryside since grasses, sagebrush, currants, and prickly pear cactus can be found.

Lichen, a moss-like plant, grows on the tower. Colors range from yellow and green to red. Climbers must be careful when it rains because the wet lichen can become very slippery.

DIRECTIONS:

Choose a marker. Flip a coin for moves:

heads—move one space

tails—move two spaces.

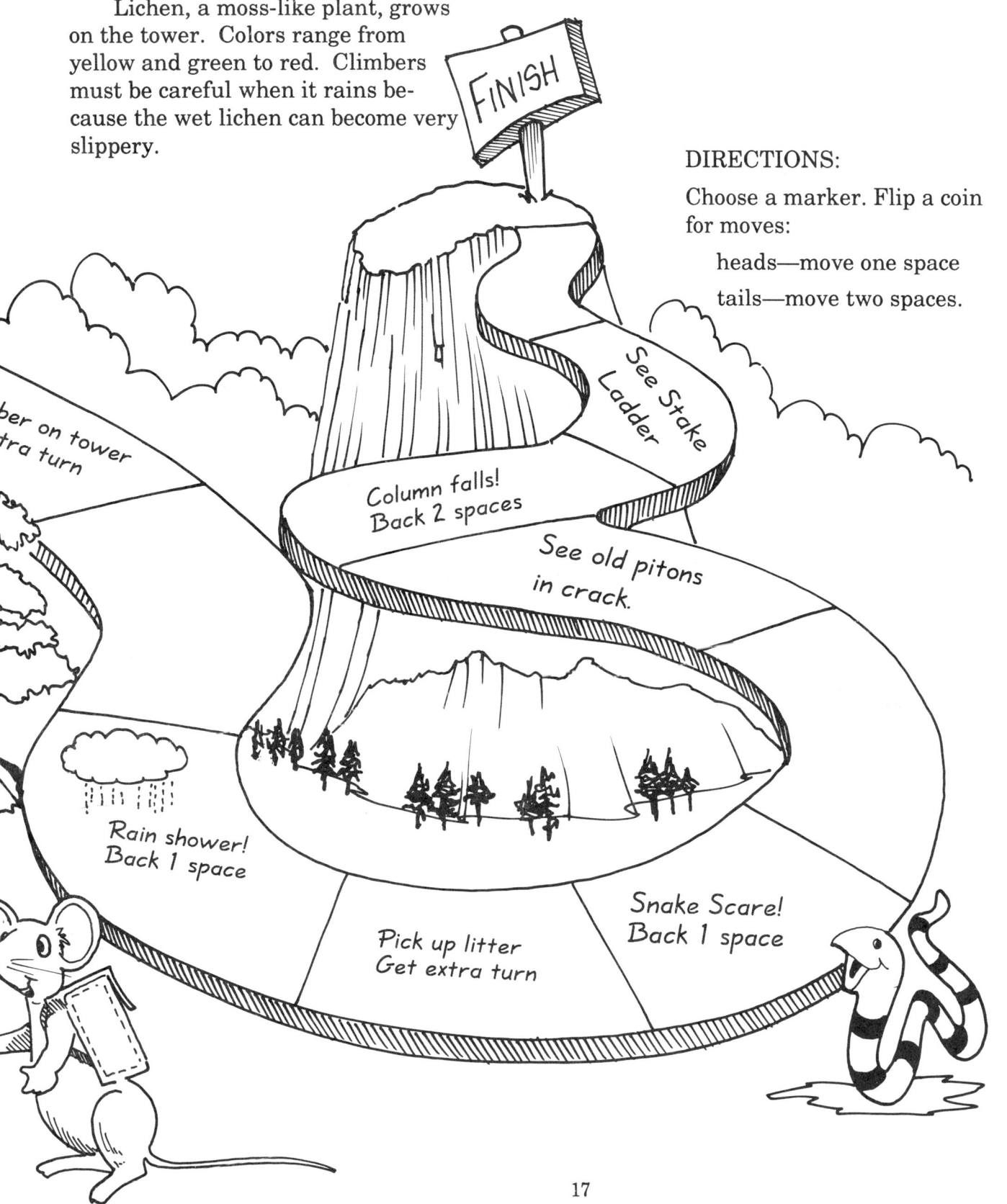

Prairie Dog Town

Did you ever wonder where prairie dogs got their name? It is curious because they do not resemble a dog at all! Prairie dogs are rodents and they belong to the squirrel family. At one time, there were many more prairie dogs than found today. Now, the animals thrive best in protected areas such as Devils Tower National Monument.

Prairie dogs are very sociable and live together in an area referred to as a town. The members of the town live in underground burrows. Several prairie dogs belong to a social group, called a **coterie**. Usually there is an adult male, three or four females, and several young members of one coterie. However, as many as thirty-nine members have been discovered.

A burrow contains many chambers. These include a listening post (close to the surface), toilet, multi-chambered living room, and a dry room. The dry room is above the living chamber and is used when the living area becomes wet due to a storm.

Insects and animals may use a deserted burrow for their home because the humidity and temperature are fairly constant and snakes may use the burrow to escape the summer heat.

Young prairie dogs are born in the Spring. They remain in the burrow and nurse for about six to seven weeks. During May or June, the pups leave the security of the burrow to explore their new surroundings. The young must learn many things about their world, such as what food to eat, how to protect themselves, and how to build a burrow.

You can help protect prairie dogs by not feeding them. The salt and preservatives added to human food can upset the prairie dog's natural water and salt balance. This might cause the prairie dogs to get very sick. They can also starve in the winter if they are accustomed to being fed by humans during the busy summer months.

You must never reach into a burrow because rattlesnakes sometimes use them to escape the summer heat. Either a rattlesnake or a prairie dog might bite you.

Remember that it is important not to disturb prairie dogs so that future generations may enjoy watching a natural, healthy prairie dog town.

LET'S DRAW A PRAIRIE DOG!

STEP 1
1. Start with some round shapes for the head and body. The dotted lines help to make your prairie dog appear round.

STEP 2
Next, add the arms, the legs, and the ear. Notice how one arm and one leg seem to be on the other side of the body.

STEP 3
Add a smile, the eye and tail. You might want to draw some trees in the background, too!

Belle Fourche River

The Belle Fourche River was called "beautiful fork" by the French fur traders of the past. Cottonwood trees line the riverbank as it winds below Devils Tower. The top of the Tower rises 1,267 feet (386 meters) above the river.

Once, the mighty river of long, long ago helped to shape the surrounding countryside and the Tower. Today, its woodland habitat supports many plants and animals that have adapted to its special environment.

Camping along the river is a favorite activity for visitors today. It was like this in the past, first among the Native Americans and then the early settlers. One old time resident is believed to have stated that he had to **ford** (cross) the river seven times before reaching the Monument camping area. He lived only ten miles by way of today's modern roads!

You may have the opportunity to see a cottontail rabbit grazing or a family of whitetail deer passing by. You may notice the redtail hawk or golden eagle soaring overhead. You definitely can't miss the music of the many birds singing their favorite songs.

CAN YOU FIND THREE THAT MATCH?

Hiking Trails and Safety Tips

There are several designated trails which help acquaint you with Devils Tower National Monument. The Tower Trail, which is 1.25 miles (2 kilometers) around the Tower, has markers and benches along the way. It is the only trail from which you will see the Tower close up.

Three other trails are longer but less crowded. They are The Red Beds, Joyner Ridge, and Valley View Trails. You can explore the different animal and plant environments as you pass the riverside habitat, the open meadows, the prairie dog town, and the pine forest.

Can you think of important safety tips to remember as you hike Devils Tower? What important items would you take with you to make your adventure a safe one?

Hikers should...hike with a friend.

...walk, not run, on trails.

...stay only on designated trails.

...bring lots of water on hot days.

...look at but not touch or harm, animals or plants.

...leave everything just as it is found.

...pack out everything they pack in.

...help by picking up litter they find along the way.

Pine Forest

The pine forest (Ponderosa Pine) grows along the higher ridge of Devils Tower. This area supports plants and animals that have adapted to its special environment, as well. For example, you may discover a red squirrel scurrying by or a porcupine meandering on its way. However, you will not find the blacktail prairie dogs here. Each species of plant and animal knows instinctly which habitat is best for its survival.

If you look closely, you may notice long, yellow marks or wounds in the trunks of many pine trees. These wounds are caused by the porcupine. The porcupine gnaws through the bark of young trees with its sharp, chisel-like teeth. The soft, inner bark of the tree is a favorite delicacy. Many young trees may not survive these attacks but, this is a way of keeping nature in balance.

DIRECTIONS: Complete the mystery drawing below. Find square #1 in the jumbled drawings and see how it is drawn in square #1 below. Now it's your turn! Find square #2 and copy what you see. Complete all the squares to discover the drawing.

Wildflowers

Wildflowers are plentiful at Devils Tower National Monument. Carpets of color are displayed for all to enjoy! Yellow (Arrowleaf Balsam root), white (Yarrow), blue (Larkspur), purple (Violet), red, pink, rose (Milkweed), and orange flowers (Scarlet Globe Mallow) can be found. Many varieties of each color are abundant.

See if you can discover the flowers of Devils Tower, but remember not to pick or disturb them!

Fold along the dotted lines to discover the mystery!

Birds of Devils Tower National Monument

More than ninety species of birds make their home at Devils Tower National Monument. The mountains and the prairies join here, so species common to both habitats can be found. Each species hunts for food in different ways and in different places. Therefore, nature allows the many varieties of birds to live in the same area without competing for survival.

Large birds of prey can be seen swooping down onto the open grasslands. See if you can recognize one of the following: red-tailed hawk, American kestrel, golden and bald eagle, prairie falcon, or the turkey vulture. Did you know the turkey vulture can have a wing span of 6 feet?

The prairie falcon, rock dove (pigeon), and the white-throated swift are the only birds that nest directly on the Tower.

Some other common Monument residents include: the white-breasted nuthatch, the mountain bluebird, the red-headed woodpecker, the meadowlark, the robin, the vireos, and the Audubon warbler.

Draw a line from each bird to its name.

BIRD MATCH

MOUNTAIN BLUEBIRD

ROCK DOVE

WESTERN MEADOWLARK

TURKEY VULTURE

ROBIN

PRAIRIE FALCON

GOLDEN EAGLE

HAIRY WOODPECKER

Wildlife Mammals

The most visible mammals at Devils Tower are the prairie dogs, the whitetail deer, and the mule deer. With luck, you may see other mammals as well. Look carefully and you may spot one or more of the following: the cottontail rabbit, least chipmunk, red squirrel, ground squirrel, porcupine, coyote, skunk, fox, raccoon, mink, muskrat, or wood rat.

| CHIPMUNK | PORCUPINE | DEER |

SNAKES

Common snakes found at Devils Tower National Monument include the bull, garter, and rattlesnake. The bull and garter snake are harmless, whereas the rattlesnake is **venomous** (poisonous).

Remember that all snakes, including the venomous ones, are useful to nature's delicate environmental balance! You should leave all snakes alone!

Do not pick up any snake and watch carefully where you step. If you happen to see a snake, stand quite still. Snakes will defend themselves if they cannot escape.

Shade the "O" dark and the "X" light.

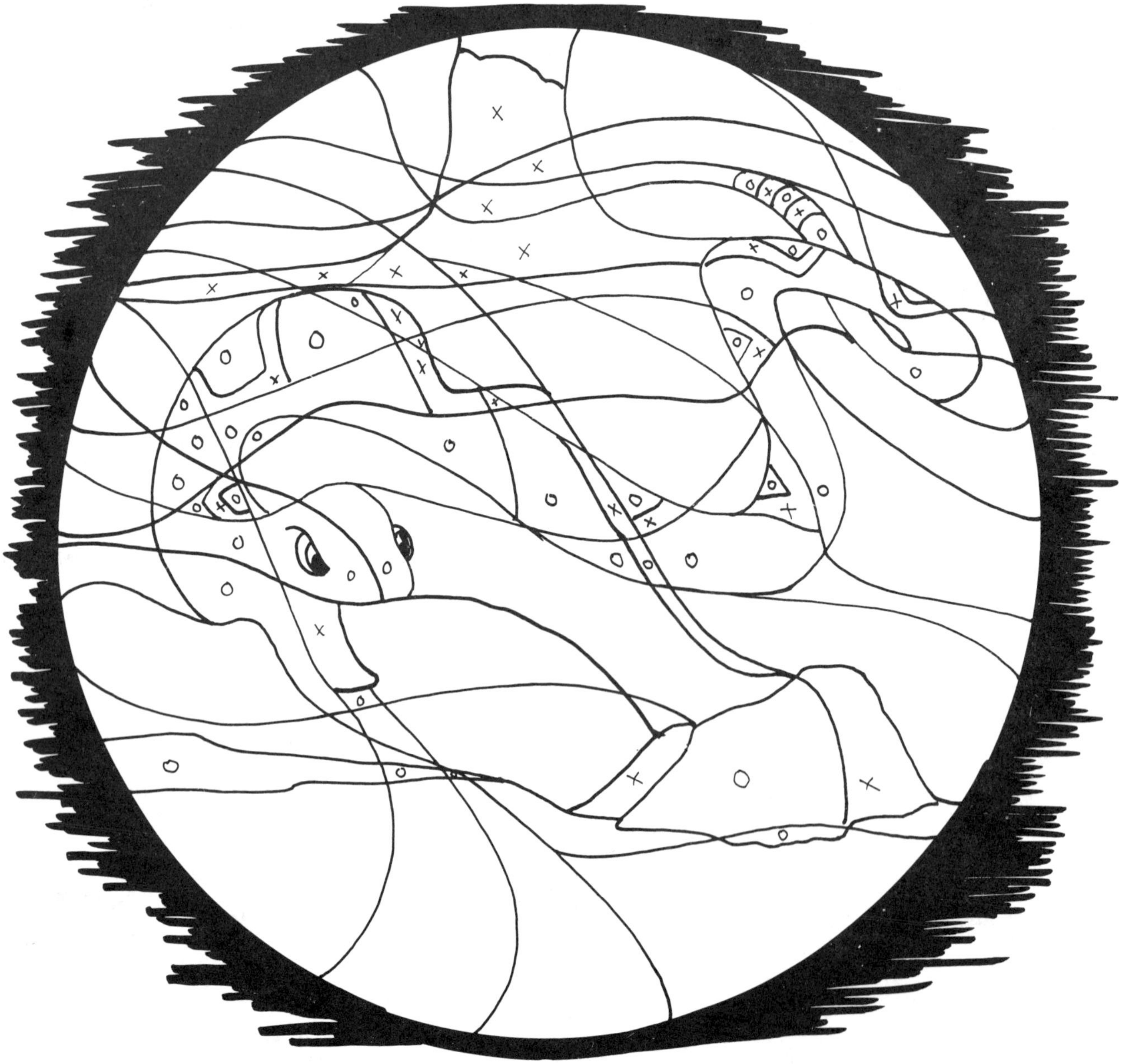

Poison Ivy and Safety Tips

Did you know that poison ivy grows as a shrub or vine? Do you know how to recognize poison ivy? Do you know where poison ivy grows?

Look for three shiny, pointed, oval, lobed or toothed leaves. The plant has white, waxy berries. The flowers are greenish-white, found in clusters around the axils of the leaves (between the stem and the leaf).

This plant is a native to the Southwest. It is found in the woodlands and along streams. The plant produces a **dermatitis** (skin irritation) which varies from one person to another, depending on the person's sensitivity. An oil-resin chemical (**urushiol**) is released upon contact, causing dermatitis. Urushiol is found in the sap which is located in all parts of the plant.

The chemical is released when the plant is touched or bruised and also can be spread by animals, dust particles, pollens, ashes, and even clothing. The chemical can remain on the clothes for years if it is not washed out!

Avoid contact with poison ivy. If you discover you have had contact, wash carefully with a strong soap within five to ten minutes to help prevent irritation. Be especially alert during spring and summer months when the plants are full of sap and easily bruised!

Recycling

Many visitors come to Devils Tower National Monument each year to enjoy its natural resources. Natural resources include animals, plants, rocks, soil, pure air, clean water, and the beautiful environment.

To preserve our natural environment, from Devils Tower National Monument to the entire world, we must make an effort to conserve and protect nature's delicate balance. By becoming aware and following simple steps, you **can** make a difference!

You can help to preserve our outdoor environment. Activities such as picking up litter, even if it is not yours, help keep the environment clean. You can help protect animals by following a "do not disturb" policy. Also, leaving the environment such as rocks and flowers, untouched preserves our resources for the future.

Other activities to consider may include: taking shorter showers to conserve water, saving paper and glass containers to use for other purposes, and buying new items which are environmentally friendly.

Recycling can help our environment and still be fun! You can make new items from used items. Follow the directions below to recycle a plastic bottle. What other items can you use to make new things?

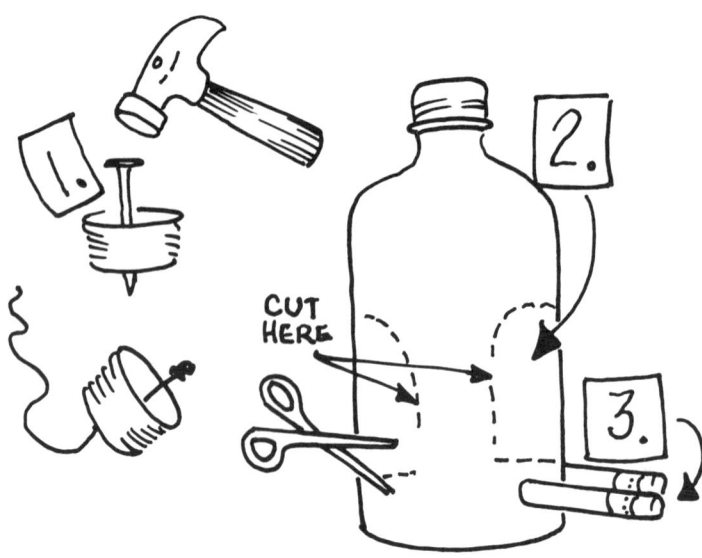

You can make a great birdfeeder and help save the environment at the same time. Begin by using a large two liter plastic soft drink bottle.

1. With a hammer and a nail, punch a hole in the cap and put a string through the hole and tie a knot so your bottle can hang.

2. Then, with an adult helping you, cut the circles out of the bottle so the birds can see the food. With a paper punch, punch holes and insert pencils for the birds to sit on while they are eating. Fill with some bird seed, hang on your patio, and have a good time and be proud that you are saving the environment.

New Words

You have learned many new words throughout this book. Some of these words are found in the word search below. See if you can solve the puzzle. Check the answer page to find out if you are correct.

FIND THESE HIDDEN WORDS!

IGNEOUS	ANCHORS
FAULTS	COTERIE
SEDIMENTARY	ASCENT
EROSION	FORD
ENVIRONMENT	DESCENT
DERMATITIS	

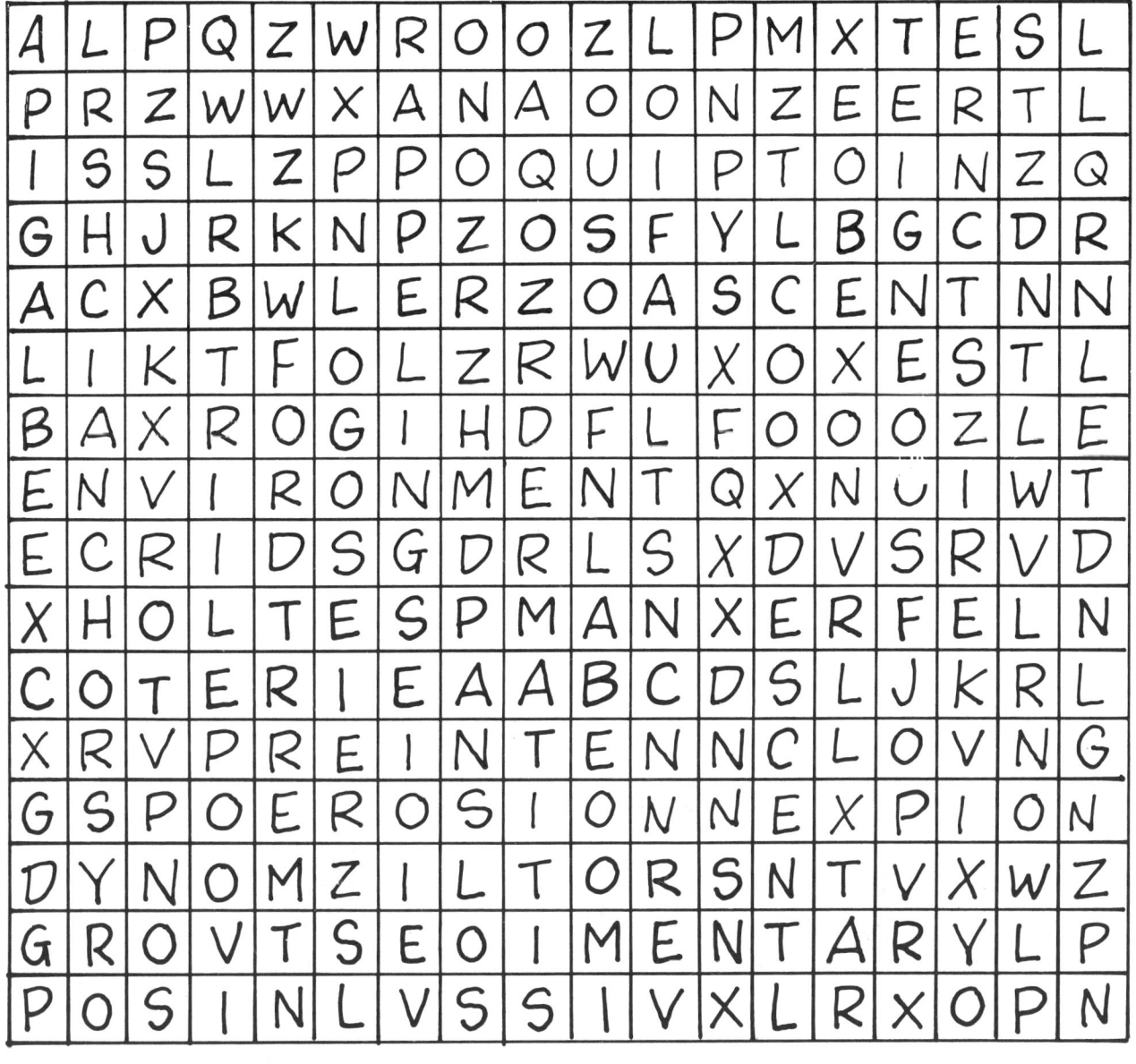

Answer Page

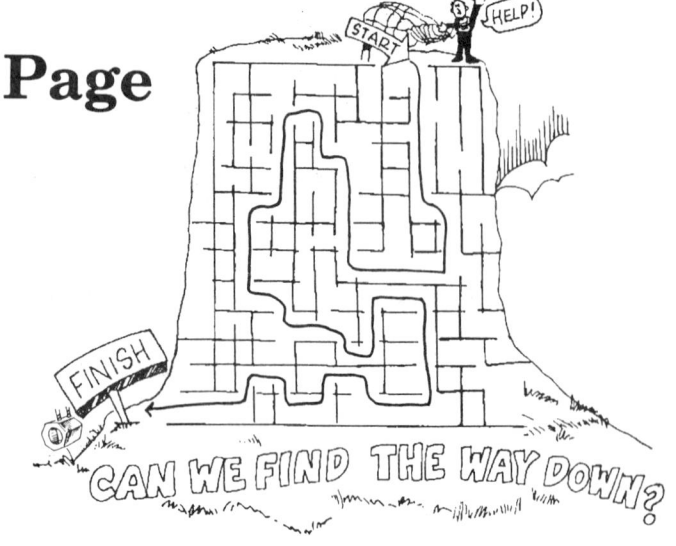

WORD LIST

WORD LIST:
Colonel Dodge
Henry Newton
homesteaders
Devils Tower
ownership
prospectors
ranches
expedition
Belle Fourche
Mateo Tepee
Black Hills

CAN WE FIND THE WAY DOWN?

DEVILS TOWER BECAME OUR FIRST MONUMENT

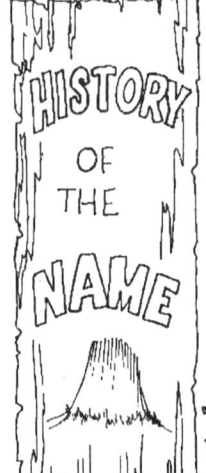

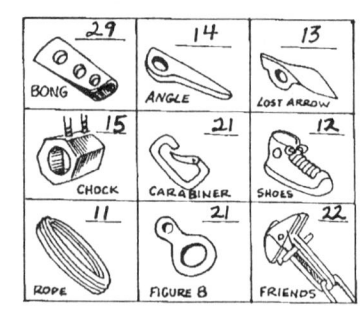

CAN YOU FIND THREE THAT MATCH?

FIND THESE HIDDEN WORDS!

IGNEOUS   ANCHORS
FAULTS   COTERIE
SEDIMENTARY ASCENT
EROSION   FORD
ENVIRONMENT DESCENT
DERMATITIS

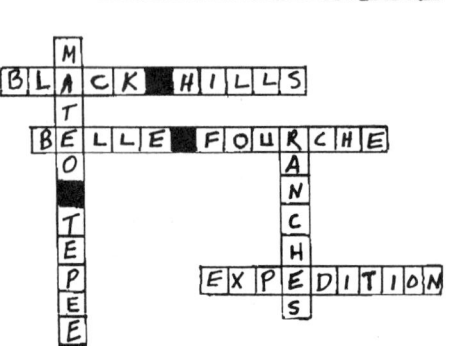

32